Also by Angela Averitt

FRANISTAN
(children's book)

THE MONEY BOOK
(children's book)

Intrepid

Intrepid

POEMS BY

Angela Averitt

Ex Press · *Eureka, California*

2007

AN EX PRESS BOOK

Copyright © 2007 by Angela Averitt
All rights reserved under International and Pan-American
Copyright Conventions. Published in the United States
By Ex Press, Eureka, CA

ISBN 978-0-6151-5991-1

Printed in the United States of America
First Edition

To Mom and Dad and Sherlock

CONTENTS

Northampton, MA

Snow Day	3
Canada	4
Church	6
Pedestrian	7
Reverie	8
Behind the State Hospital	9

New York

Miracle	13
Not That	15
That Way	16
Times Square	17
Sky	18
Later	19

Miami

Jana	23
Striped	24
Spoken	26

Eureka, CA

Remembering	29
Exchange	30
Room	31
Said	32
Routine	33
Set Down	34
Telling Time	35
Walking at Night	36
Infinity	37
Tools	38
Also There	39
Renewal II	40
Serene	41

Northampton, MA

Snow Day

It was the radio personality
Who called it first to me,
But the thick icy loaves on
The window sill that
Proved the words: snow day.
The dreams of a hallowed
Sleep had tapped out to
Leave this wonderment of
Rescheduling where finally
One's real life: sledding,
Neighbor friends, ice skating
In the streets in boots and
Back-born angels in the snow
Had kicked all false
Pretenses into tomorrow
And awoken a world of children
To slippery slopes, wet
Mittens, cocoa and
The news that all was
Not lost in the known
World, nor all known
In this one.

Canada

Lying in a grassy park in Quebec
The darkly handsome young man
Looks up and says, dreamily,
"There are no clouds in Canada."
We laugh, our little group of four—
Just out from childhood.

We are swimmers
And this is the first time out of
Our country for most of the
Teenagers who rode
Ten hours on the bus.
We are more than swimmers,
And less, too.
We are off the bus in the foreign
Country for the first time and
We are happy to be together.

They are all better swimmers
Than I am and will most likely
Win their races,
But I am not awed by Canada.
I have already been other places,
Really foreign places like France
And Greece.
France, though, had felt like a
Welcoming embrace, right
Down to the testy old lady
Who slapped at my hand
As I tried to pick a pear at the
Market. "No touch!"

And I knew her,
Because I am the same.
(She probably could not even
Swim at all.)
Surely, at the threshold of

Growing up
I understood the way of
Testy people with something
To guard and I could smile and
Want the pears more for her
Protective care.
But here, with the lovely
Young man, with Canada
Without clouds,
Without the familiarity
Of house and home,
I laughed,
And loved,
But knew I could
Not beat them—
The Canadians.

I knew that I had
Not come to win
But to explain
And truly,
The moment
Came when,
Walking along the neat
Large square tiles in
Shiny blue Lycra bathing suits,
To my dearest female friend,
When the Canadian girl
Could say only,
"De temps en temps"
I was able to say:
Occasionally or
From time
To time.

Church

No, I won't say to you:
You aren't Episcopalian—
Because you certainly sit on that thinly cushioned seat
Each week.

Though sometimes we visit everything we aren't—
Straying only from what we know of home.
From where can you leave if not from home?

Anything else is a show with its price of entry
(Free-for-all or some sumptuous affair matters not;
When you leave a show you leave it all
Except for some small trinket to trinkle on the way home.)

When I left that door for the last time it was said
(I suppose, just as it was said every time)
About the peace which (passes/passeth) passethes
Understanding and was to keep my heart, my mind...

Out of that door we run with peace
As the thin bench-marked line pushes back out
From the back of the thighs.
Why are the doors so heavy on a church?
Thick slabs of wood are good for carving
While cold winter days forget the faithful.

Pedestrian

The grey cement wall
Comes only to my shoulder
But it follows my path
All the way down the hill
And turns into the little
Arched bridge as it bows
Over the creek.

Just after the bridge
I make the sharp left
Off of the sidewalk of
Cement squares
And into the woods.

The bigger river, the real one,
Flows here and it is unbridged,
But the downed tree has
Come to span it as a make-shift one.

The dirt path rises tens of feet above the full spring river
And I can smell the rushing water.
The smell and the sound are fresh
And bring the thought of possibilities
To mind. Even the path
Is muddy and there's an excitement to
Its narrowness and height above the water.

This is a small river, though,
And a small town. There surely are not
Many who've looked it
So carefully
Up and down.

Reverie

The maple grove is filled with snow
And summer's petals long since gone—
The trees are stark their colors done
Through some dear dream of flight.

The days are cold and short and tight
Now winter's long tirade is here—
There's barely any rest from fears
On long cold nights and icy morns.

There was a time in middle June
When frost could not a crystal grow
And light did flood the western skies
To make one want to dream awake.

Back in those days we played a fool
And sat up late with lemonade
To watch the eve outshine the moon
And bask in reason's favor.

But favor's gone in winter's coat
And nothing warms the limbs but work.
There are no fruits left on the vines
Then surely every heart repents on

Desperate nights and biting days
When bitterness stays buttoned up
Against all tasks like well-worn sacks
Of dried-out beans on shelves unburdened now.

Behind the State Hospital

The trail that leads to the river slopes only slightly and is long.
The flowers along both sides are gloriously lively
And the dogs that poke a cold nose at my dog are friendly,
Their people quiet and gruff.

The hill beside the path fills up with dogs, in fact,
Who scramble and cut in some mock tournament
Avoided by the people who huddle on the side
On a mid-afternoon of a dry summer's day.

After only the briefest stay I must coax my own swift dog onward.
We walk away from the gathering hill and walk
Along the river, though far above, having taken the path on the left.
The right side leads down river and off to the playing fields.

This day we follow the path down along the steep bank
To skirt the cornfields and then up through the woods
And around again to the pocked dirt lot where the car is parked.
The corn is still short. It is the best marker of time I know in summer.

These grounds have been walked for hundreds of years,
A century ago by those seeking healing…
The brick buildings loom empty on the hill two fields back.
The place was started as a country retreat for mental relief.

The place exists for us now as a walking retreat.
But it is sold again and will be neatly cut yards with small houses.
The cornfields will be yards and driveways,
Private retreats for private lives.

Maybe there are blessings over the place
Left by those who healed, or tried, or left or died here.
Maybe the place has always soothed, was chosen for such effects.
They blared Mozart from the buildings, ate cheese to say goodbye.

The place is unusual, eerie, peaceful, lush and desired.
The corn grows well here, as do the pumpkins.
The houses will be coveted.
The river still watches, I suppose, and passes without a word.

Mental relief?
By the river, or a field, a gathering, a game,
A hospital, a home...
They'll settle if they can; we'll walk some other woods.

New York

Miracle

Late 1995, probably fall,
In that little apartment with the
Polished golden wood floors
And the tight kitchen with the
White-painted table I'd found
On the street—
Had everything in there come
Off of the street?
It was so far uptown
(New York City, of course)
That we were in our own
World of temples
And bakeries
And mostly just apartment
Buildings
(All, it seemed, so much
Nicer than mine)—
And in this neighborhood
The people owned cars
And the last ones
Circled for hours sometimes
To find the open spaces
To leave them for the evening.
But this was morning and
A Saturday, too,
Probably,
But maybe even a Wednesday
Morning because, I think,
I had already quit my job,
And it was a good job,
But I was finally back to myself
And also on my way out.
And leaving the apartment
I walked down the hall
I had walked, what?
500? 5000 times?
(Someone must know...

I would like to know things
Like this...)
But this time was the best time
Because I now first saw it—
The light, the beam of sunlight
Cutting across my path
And all that was in it and
All that comes from it
And simple as it was
(The simplicity may be the
Miracle of miracles—
Because—see! How
Complex...)
And even at that moment
(Which is rare sometimes)
I thought right then,
This is a miracle—
The light shaft shown in
The window of a shaft—
The center of our building having
A hollow core but not so
Lovely as to be able to say courtyard—
Still, there it was,
The thing in itself,
The opening of the eyes—
The thought,
Word
And deed.

Not That

I'm not writing about that,
Or that, although I was
Alive for both.
I'm writing about the
Journey the heart makes
In the small choices—
Like whether to hold the head
Up or down or
The hands palms up or
Palms down...
And why you set the place
With that glass and
Who made it?
And why they went to
The wax factory day after day
And why OSHA says
That it's okay
As long as the chemicals
Aren't too toxic.
Somewhere we learn to mourn
The tragic face but what
Scratch of nails
Came first?

That Way

That way left everything greenish
And blurred, unsolid. There
Was real solitude there, but
We had to work too hard and
Words broke everything then.
Besides that the words flooded in
And the fault line landed there
Between in and out of love.
Beyond that there was red and
Still green but it fit in the
Mix and then all those
Words regained the numbers
Of fruits and money—still
The loss was the foreignness and
Bitter death of the past...and the
Brutality woven in.
It would be years before blue
Returned in all its likeness of
Everything free, clear and infinite.
That way was unforeseeable
To someone with skies in her eyes
Pinned up with absence and love.

Times Square

The young man is shifting
Paper cups, lifting them up
And putting them down.
His hand moves slowly, then faster,
Faster as he shuffles the cups—
Lifting less and less.
His friend is finding the yellow ball
Each time. He makes it look easy.
The crowd has gathered and
We watch as the man in
A bright blue Dolphin's jacket
Shuffles, as the man in the
Black and orange leather jacket wins.
So gaily the one hands
A twenty to the gamer,
So quickly he wins and sees
Two twenties handed back.
The player bets again—
Both bills this time—
Any of us can see the yellow ball
And so does the player and gets
Four twenties back.
Now a woman in a black dress coat
Steps in. She has twenty dollars.
I can't look; I pull away
From the group on the corner.
"It's fixed, it's fixed,"
One wants to say,
Just like a crowd
Is anyway.

Sky

About your dream of the Skylark Pavilion
With the accident victim lying there,
And the police who wouldn't come
And the apartment floors too fatigue and too forest green,
With the sunken tub with the good view I say:

See that pierced darkness of the early evening
February sky

Small pinpoints of light are floating
Over your head
Even now

Later

Later that same day
I walked across Houston Street
And past Saint Anthony's
And even later the large

Boulevards and the narrow straight
Slices across became full of
The smells of chicken broth and
Garbage and the ever present

Exhaust from the autos—
And much, much later
I was floating face up in the
Bright blue of the Atlantic—

Miami Beach, 1996,
And that water was warm, warm
Like salty bath water and
Just three feet out it was

Three feet deep and I could
Float like I was at a spa
And so were all the other women
And the old and pudgy ones

Sat while the young and taut ones
Walked and all that finding
And all that losing from
Saint Anthony's to Coney Island

Was drifting out to sea
On the warm January waves.
We never said goodbye—
But you would say "later,"

Later for the lost,
Later for the found,

Later drifting off,
Lifting off from
Sand-down ground.

Miami

Jana

Don't sit on that porch rail;
Don't wait for us in that
Way. While we sang and
Played there you would never
Sing but only reappear and
Would maybe have said: Put
It back—put back my world—
But in those days they
Were already in state with us
And, Jana, we couldn't have
Stopped for anything then—
Still the war came and
Where is there left to sit?
Because I don't see
That country without a
Porch and I don't think
We've grown up fast enough
To know that water lets
The river run and that day
Of encampment and decision
Is not spoken out
In foreign speech.

Striped

Elements of striped attire
Strewn so thickly into the
Closet and down the hall,
One is left to wonder what
Outfits, personalities or
Bravados the young women
Have not acquired, worn out or
Tried on...but this day there
Is nothing to wear, like there
Wasn't anything right for
Yesterday and this is the way
It may feel for years to come.
Why waste the years on
Plastic candle holders,
Grocery store jobs and
Dangling earrings? Why spend
Another day practicing tennis
Or music or art?

                Except that
Collage was a wonder to behold
Which was clipped painstakingly
From real photos as well as
Magazine images and with
Colors, stripes, writing...
This was the location of the
Life of that one who could
Not lift a shirt from the floor
(That would have been
Something too decisive
To survive)—
                a gratuitous
Collage that more than covered
The wall and spread also to
Window and floor with its
Ravenous colors and extremes
Of love. The young

Have their methods of
Survival that the
Old ones have long
Forgotten...after all,
Several wars, accidents,
Earthquakes, hurricanes
And operations later,
Life slows to itself
And one must eventually
Consider that while
There never was anywhere
That fit those clothes,
Still death is not so
Greedy for most of
Us, either. The hollow
Cry of the striped shirt
Notwithstanding, even
One's young life is not
Full of preparation—
Count not those
Lines to lengthen out
To nothing, as in default,
And empty floors festoon
Out to shape the way to
Retrieval or recollection.

Spoken

Your father was in his 70s
And you still just 21—
And he spoke of God
And writings about God
In Italian for hours.
I would have listened to him
For days and accepted your
Kindness as you sat
Beside him and brought
His words to me in English
In your light Spanish accent.
How much this white-haired man
Doted upon his only child,
How relieved I felt to find
A man loved you this much—
How grateful, also, I was
To finally hear
Wisdom coming out of your mouth.
You'd only spoken of Spain
And your mother,
Whom I'd never met—
But then here had arrived
This grandfatherly man
To fix under the sink
And light the lamps
In your home
With his love of God
And of his daughter.

Eureka, CA

Remembering

It's not for you—
Though you were there—
Well, okay, it is but—
Not in that way...
Because, yes—I will
Show up but I don't
Know who put this
Perfect photo of an ocean
In front of me...
And there is no explanation
That could lead to such
Lovely condensing of this
Beauty into a view—
A morning view that
Rightfully I did not
Come to see...So
The undeserved reward
Was shockingly high and
There was no card
Attached.

Exchange

We walk through the park and talk.
You tell me unimaginable things
That I believe since
They come from you.

I told you once that I was
Tired of clichés and
These sorts of generalizations—
But you calmly said
You tell me things simply
And I should be glad about that.

I am glad about that—
And simple as they are
You often have to tell me
Again and again before I
Remember and even so,
I may not really know
For—what? Months? Days?
Years? These are open secrets,
You say, in that you tell them
To those who listen.

"Open secrets?" I think.
The irony is: It often feels smarter
Before I start to know.

Room

The empty room is full of
Possibility, and much is built
Or created here.
The walls recede when approached,
Though, so don't believe the French
Philosophers or ancients who will
Tell you they have touched them.
They have not touched the walls,
But may want you to try it, just
To know that the place, untouchable,
Is also a place most acceptable,
But will never be
Accepted here.

Said

It's just English—that's all.
(Or any known language either...)
You want to say:
Nic nic nigh un dee beetle bop
But have to say "as is" and
"Therefore" and "this way"
When all you really want
To say is: nee my nee on dee
Bop bop. Occasionally
You may play Spanish radio
And think that that is closer
(And it is) but even so they
Have to sputter and pop eventually too,
(We all do.)
And then you turn the channel.
(Don't blame yourself—
It's in there...it's just not
Coming out smoothly. We
Turn those corners
Making maps and
Try to remember the first
By the last before the
Sputtering makes
Us stop.)

Routine

Routine is for old folks.
Does it make us old?
Or do the old make it?
Efficiently the same
Either way
It is in the routine
That we make up the day,

Like the patterns that we see,
Like the sun's heady arc,
Dispelling the
Lost meanings of
The cold and the dark.

Set Down

When you call be sure and include your address.
When you fall measure an insured redress.
When you loll treasure an issued red dress.
When you alter your uninsured rent, rest.
When new ulterior one inch erred, re-interest.
Winnow out or win a cheery in trust.
We know how to win our tree into us.
We know how to win aren't we into us?
Winnow in the wind, are we intuitive?
Trust, re-trust, intuit in the cherry trees, and win, re-won.

Telling Time

Stretching, scratching, eking out the morning time,
The sun comes up to scatter clouds away.
It is the first cool morning in days;
It is the first morning anyone can remember
When the rain did not agitate the mind or

The wind play roughly with the branches and blooms.
This day is the first day of the miraculous reformation of the world.
Who would be the first one to come?
Surely this very house will disappear into smoke by evening.

We will hang our heads to think of the deals we made.
Our hearts will drop to recall how long we waited, and how
We wandered far and were hungry...were we tired?
Then, in the inhaling of a breath, everything rushes back
Into our sight and we all fall backwards, laughing.
This is the scene we remember, the one we remember waiting for,
The one we remember thinking of when we first thought of home.

Walking at Night

Stark white and small clouds light the dark sky—
Piercingly bright stars point through the blue night—

This is darkness
With color
With light and white...
Shapes of clouds reflect a light source unseen.

On that darkest night with all the street lights,
House lights out
There was a source of light—
It shone up from the earth to light
White underbelly,
Miraculous skies.

Infinity

Take this down:

There will not be any cupcakes,
So don't expect it—

I don't even know if you are the cupcake
Expecting kind but

After all these years,
And times...

Still,
One might sit on a log

Next to you
And overlooking some

Dark waters

In a town, but...
How could anything compare

To this now?
At once so bright

And piercingly cold?

Tools

The power is out first thing Thursday morning—
Unusual to wake and see darkness on the clock's face.

I attempt to fix the power outage myself.
I look in my tool box at all the sundries I have acquired:
Old, rusted, chipped, inherited bits of patience,
Small amounts of endurance.

There are hand tools in the box as well:
Crushers askew in there with
Resignation and various sanders
Like old hopes and worn questions.
The box could be labeled:
"Not the right tools for the job."
This would apply to nearly any job.

Still, on this drizzly morning I find myself
Poking through the old will drivers
And the broken circular reasonings until I find
Some hand-worn apathy I could use.

The garage door must be opened by hand.
I drive the car to the park, walk the dog.
By the time we return, the power is back on.
Faithful old tools have brought us
Again to the world of power and light.
This is the extent of our handiness just yet.

Also There

There are growing on the jagged borders of long-since tended yards
A spiked sort of daisy, but foreign to the white/yellow domesticated,
Soft-petaled, fried-egg type...
Rather, these are stark daisies with pointed rays of blood orange,
Reds and ambers which seem in a rage between open and closed...

Some ragged, inhospitable movement moves the shape and color,
If not the spears themselves:
Not daisies, not thorns—a pointed in-between, some long forgotten
Taste of curled retreat, reluctant pursuit that bursts a way
Near aged cement, old rocks, broken bricks,
Cracked steps and walks.

Renewal II

Monday,
This day,
Set in fall,
Opens just
A sliver...

This day small light
Peers through rough skies
To look at us

Sitting here
Collecting
Pieces of sorrow
Pieces of small dreams

That fell apart in the rain
That scattered in the night
Shards easily brought in now,

Shards of colored went-wrong,
In fists of no more fight.

Serene

Bright and sharp translucent little bubbles
Rise and burst into helmets of water.
Little beads play upon the leaves
And sharp grasses taunt the sides of the path on the marsh.

This is the place to which all waste is finally swept
Marking the reluctant steps of decay.
The passerby feels the damp air, the pond, the dew and bubbles;
Even the smell of loss is sweet.

Nothing here is lost, of course. The signs in the center
Would inform the school child of the cyclical nature of nature.
The clever wooden wheels turn round with a crank on the display,
Though nothing else would move so well.

Loss is sensible here, defying those neat words.
Fall really is gone. So is winter.
Spring meticulously devours the old as does rot and decay.
This isn't the world we picked apart last year.

The remembered world comes back now only in bird song or twitter.
That old pond has mulched and seeped and risen
And is, by now, frozen in northern ice, flowing to islands, and
Baked into the silent walls of some faraway sculpted garden.

Such an old world we awaken to find gone—
Rotted, sunken, drifted,
Gone while we slept through the cold and the storms
And the darkness of rain.

It isn't early morning now;
All the rush of early growth is gone—
What is left will be our summer without regrets,
Will touch our misty trails come fall.

A NOTE ABOUT THE AUTHOR

Angela Averitt graduated from Williams College and Bank Street College of Education. She taught first and second grades in New York City, high school in Eureka, California, and at Humboldt State University. Her poetry has appeared in *California Quarterly* and *Red Wheelbarrow.*

www.ingramcontent.com/pod-product-compliance
Lightning Source LLC
Chambersburg PA
CBHW032113040426
42337CB00040B/555